What Am I Going to Be?

I have a furry,
brown coat.
I have long,
sharp claws.
What am I?

2

I have a long,
golden mane.
I have soft,
velvet paws.
What am I?

6

7

I am a
leaping lion.

9

I have shiny,
sharp teeth.
I have a long,
lashing tail.
What am I?

10

11

I am a
creepy crocodile.

12

13

I have a row
of purple spikes.
I have shiny,
silver scales.
What am I?

14

15

I am a
dreadful dragon.

I have wild,
rolling eyes.
I have lots of
spots and dots.
What am I?

18

I am a
munching monster.

21

Put us all together,
and what do you have?

23

You have a play!